KENT STATE UNIVERS   IO

W9-BXM-196

PUEBLO BOY

PUEBLO BOY

Growing Up in Two Worlds

MARCIA KEEGAN

COBBLEHILL BOOKS
Dutton   New York

Dedicated to the memory
of J.D. Roybal
of San Ildefonso Pueblo

Copyright © 1991 by Marcia Keegan
All rights reserved. No part of this book may be
reproduced in any form without permission in writing
from the publisher.

Library of Congress Cataloging-in-Publication Data
Keegan, Marcia.
Pueblo boy / Marcia Keegan ; photographs by the author. p. cm.
Summary: Text and photographs depict the home, school, and
cultural life of a young Indian boy growing up on the San Ildefonso
Pueblo in New Mexico.
ISBN 0-525-65060-1
1. Roybal, Timmy. 2. Pueblo Indians—Biography—Juvenile
literature. 3. Pueblo Indians—Social life and customs—Juvenile
literature. 4. San Ildefonso (N.M.)—Social life and customs—
Juvenile literature. [1. Roybal, Timmy. 2. Pueblo Indians—
Biography. 3. Pueblo Indians—Social life and customs. 4. Indians
of North America—New Mexico—Biography. 5. Indians of North
America—New Mexico—Social life and customs.] I. Title.
E99.S213R695 1991 978.9′00497—dc20
[B] [92] 90-45187 CIP AC

Published in the United States by Cobblehill Books,
an affiliate of Dutton Children's Books, a division of Penguin Books USA Inc.
Designed by Jean Krulis
10 9 8 7
Printed in Hong Kong

Timmy Roybal is a ten-year-old Pueblo Indian boy. Besides doing the things that any other ten-year-old boy would do, Timmy follows the traditions of his Native American heritage.

Timmy's Indian name is Agoyo-Paa, which means "Star Fire." He received this name when he was five months old from an elder of the tribe. It had come to the elder during the Deer Dance. Timmy uses this name for all Indian ceremonies.

When the Spanish explorers first came to New Mexico and Arizona in the 1500s, they found the Native Americans living in villages. The Spanish called these villages pueblos, meaning "small towns." It is from this that the Pueblo Indians got their name.

Timmy lives at the San Ildefonso Pueblo, which is twenty-two miles north of Santa Fe, New Mexico, on the east bank of the Rio Grande. His pueblo lies between the massive peaks of the Jemez and the Sangre de Cristo mountains. The six hundred Indians of the pueblo live in one-story adobe houses.

The village looks much the same as it has for hundreds of years. Many of the houses are built of the sun-baked mud and straw mixture, called adobe. The houses look and feel like part of the earth.

From his house, Timmy can see Black Mesa, which is the home of his ancestral spirits. The people of San Ildefonso believe that

spirits live in the earth, the sky, and the waters, and in special sacred places. They believe that Chavayo, the protector spirit, lives in Black Mesa. Chavayo protects the children from harm, but also visits when they misbehave.

Timmy rides his bike to school. There are fourteen San Ildefonso children in his fifth-grade class at the day school of the pueblo. The school has classes from kindergarten through the sixth grade. The students in Timmy's class made up this list of rules and punishments at the beginning of the school year.

Rules

No teasing.

No tattle tails.

No littering.

Do not interrupt the person who is talking.

Raise your hand if you have a thought or question.

Work turned in on time.

Punishment

① name on board — warning

② 20 minutes off recess - 1st check

③ 10 minutes off P.E. - 2nd check

④ Student writes note home to parents, and to person that was bothered. Madelon adds comments. -3rd check

After he finishes sixth grade, Timmy will probably go to St. Catherine's Indian School in Santa Fe. His brother, Gary Alan, goes there and comes home on the weekends.

Timmy and his classmates do much of their schoolwork on computers.

After school, Timmy plays with his cousins Darlene, Francine, and Baby De. He calls them the "Tewa Terrors." Tewa is the native language of the San Ildefonso people. It is one of the five languages spoken by the Pueblo Indians dating back to prehistoric times. Timmy shows Baby De his Walkman and entertains them with his "Freddy" imitation, while Francine laughs happily.

Timmy loves sports and looks forward to baseball season. There is a baseball field at the pueblo where Timmy and his friends play against other Little League baseball teams from nearby pueblos.

Timmy's favorite pastimes are pocket pool, which he plays at home, and fishing at a nearby pond.

Many of Timmy's relatives are involved in the arts. Timmy's father, Gary Roybal, is a curator for the Museum of Indian Arts and Culture in Santa Fe. He shows Timmy some paintings in the museum collection that were done by Timmy's grandfather J.D. Roybal, and his great-uncle Alfonso Roybal, both famous painters.

Timmy's mother, Marie Roybal, weaves traditional ceremonial belts used in dances. She works on a handmade wooden loom in their home. Marie is a computer programmer in Santa Fe.

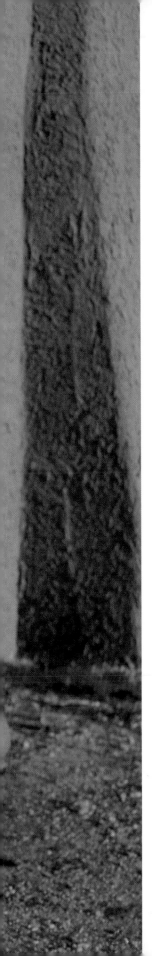

Leon Roybal, Timmy's uncle, carves kachina dolls. The kachina dolls represent spirits that communicate with living people and serve as messengers to the gods. Timmy examines the kachina doll that his uncle is working on.

This traditional kachina doll was carved by a Hopi at his village in Arizona fifty years ago. It represents a rain spirit that will provide a good harvest and a good future.

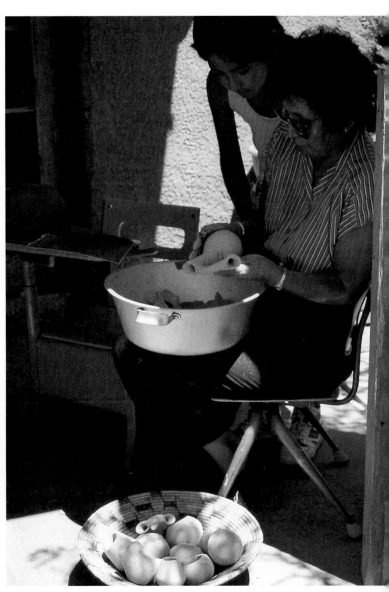

San Ildefonso is world famous for the beautiful black pottery made by the women of the pueblo. Timmy's grandmother Julia Roybal is among those women who make this distinctive Indian pottery.

She shapes the pot as she gently turns it. Next, it will be sun-dried, sanded, painted, and finally, fired outdoors.

The women of the village bake bread in outdoor ovens called
hornos, just as their ancestors did. After the wood fire inside burns
out, the ashes are removed, and the dough is placed into the oven
to bake. The adobe oven remains hot enough to bake the bread
even though there is no fire.

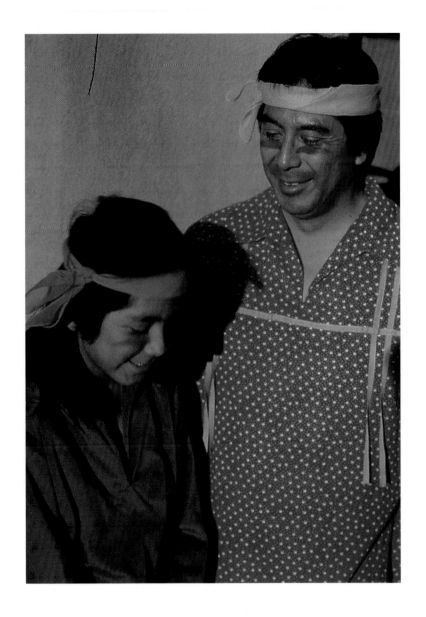

Timmy learns songs, dances, and ways of his Indian heritage from his father. Since the rituals and beliefs of the Pueblo Indians are spoken and sung but not written down, this process of father handing down the traditions to his son keeps the culture alive. Timmy will teach what he is learning to his children.

Gary Roybal teaches Timmy a Tewa prayer which translates, "Remember who you are, where you come from, and where you are going."

Pueblo Indians are identified through membership in one of the hundred clans, groups named for various symbols. There is a Bear Clan, a Parrot Clan, a Sun Clan, a Fire Clan, a Winter Clan. Clan membership is passed down through the mother. Timmy was born into the Corn Clan. Each clan is responsible for different ceremonies and dances which the Pueblo Indians believe help maintain the balance of nature.

The Pueblo Indians consider the sun, earth, moon, stars, wind, water, lightning, thunder, and all living things sacred. Since they are mostly desert farming communities, people sing and dance to make rain fall, to make crops grow, to give thanks for the crops and health, and to cure illness.

In the desert any moisture in the clay earth is deep underground. The ancient Pueblo Indians planted a special variety of corn with long roots that could reach the moisture, and short, tough leaves that could withstand wind and drought.

Traditionally, corn is the foundation of Pueblo Indian life. Without it, their ways could not have survived. In olden days, it may have accounted for as much as 80 percent of the native diet and was regarded with deep respect and reverence. Hardly a ceremony exists that does not use corn or cornmeal in some way. Since corn and other crops can't grow without water, rain dances and other practices and prayers to bring rain are a regular part of Pueblo life.

Juan Cruz Roybal, Timmy's great-grandfather, taught Timmy how to plant corn like his ancestors. He used to tell stories and sing songs. Although he understood English and Spanish, he talked mostly in Tewa. He died at the age of ninety-four, and now appears to Timmy in his dreams.

There are nineteen different Pueblo tribes in New Mexico, and they speak five different languages. There are villages such as San Ildefonso Pueblo, Taos Pueblo, and Santa Clara Pueblo. Besides Tewa, the language of the San Ildefonso Pueblo, Pueblo Indians speak Tiwa, Towa, Keresean, and Zuni.

One of Timmy's grandmothers, Margaret Tenorio, comes from the Cochiti Pueblo. She now lives on the Santa Domingo Pueblo, which is eighty miles from Timmy's home. When a Pueblo woman marries, she moves to her husband's village.

Gary Alan and Timmy like to visit Bandelier National Monument where their ancestors once lived. It is a long-abandoned Indian village, ten miles from their home. Timmy wonders what it was like when his people used to live there. Although deserted since the 1500s, many tourists visit Bandelier today.

All pueblos, even the most ancient, had a special room known as the *kiva*. It was different from ordinary dwelling areas. It was usually larger, often circular, and placed in an important area of the pueblo. Much of the religious activity of the pueblo took place in the kiva. The dancers still go there to prepare for the dances. Public parts of the ceremonies are held in the plazas, but the private portions are held in the kiva. Timmy's village kiva is in the middle of the central plaza.

Right across from the kiva is the pueblo's church. Pueblo Indians combine their ancestral beliefs with their Roman Catholic faith.

The first church was built in the 1600s, and rebuilt in 1964 on the same site. Timmy's grandfather and great-grandfather are buried in the churchyard.

The Pueblo Indian spiritual life is based on a yearly cycle tied to the agricultural growing seasons. Corn Dances are held in the spring and fall, and during the winter animal dances like the Deer and Buffalo dances are held.

The Indians of San Ildefonso perform the Corn Dance in September in honor of Saint Anthony. They bring the statue of the saint out of the church to watch the dance.

Timmy has been dancing since he was three years old. So has Gary Alan, his brother. Here his mother helps his brother get ready for a dance. The dances are prayers and everyone joins in.

"When I was two years old, my dad took me to the kiva for the first time. My first dance at age three was the Corn Dance. We grow up with dancing. My father told me about what 'chants' or prayers mean. We practice for a week before each dance."

The Green Corn Dance is a day-long ceremony thanking nature for blessings that enable the tribe to survive in harmony with the earth. The Indians believe that by dancing they preserve the continuity of the seasons and the fruitfulness of the earth.

Before the dance, the Indians purify themselves by ritual bathing and by gathering in the kiva. When they emerge from the kiva in their costumes, headdresses, and body paint, they resemble the spirits they are invoking.

Current issues are brought into the ceremony by runners who arrive from the four directions. They tell the dancers news, and the information and problems are discussed. In this way the past

and the present are represented as important to the dance. The old men of the tribe stand in a circle and chant, to the accompaniment of drums, which symbolize the heartbeat of the earth.

Timmy describes the dance. "We dance holding evergreen branches from a spruce tree. A fox tail is placed at the back, and bells on the feet. Everyone wears turquoise, especially the women, who wear lots of jewelry. We wear parrot feathers in our hair. When everyone dances, you hear the sounds of the bells ringing together.

"My favorite dance is the Corn Dance. There are over fifty members of my family from the Corn Clan of the Santa Clara and San Ildefonso pueblos dancing.

"The Corn Dance lasts all day. In the morning I wear a yellow scarf for the sun, and in the afternoon, I wear a red scarf for the sunset.

"Before dancing, I get a little nervous. My legs start shaking, but they settle down once I am dancing. When I am dancing, I feel I am part of everything."

Because Timmy has relatives belonging to different pueblos, he is eligible to participate in the dances at their pueblos. Timmy and his father also take part in the Comanche Dance, which is held each year on the feast of the patron saint of San Ildefonso, January 23.

The dance began in the early 1800s, when the Comanche Indians and the Pueblo people did a lot of trading. The Comanches would camp out near the pueblo, and the people would get together to teach each other songs. These shared songs became part of a ceremonial dance at the pueblo.

Here the chorus of drummers and singers carry the beat of the prayers and songs which relate to the earth, the sky, the rain, the clouds, and the four directions—north, south, east, and west. Timmy's father is lead dancer in the Comanche Dance.

Timmy's mother and grandmother go into the kiva to take food to the dancers during the rest period.

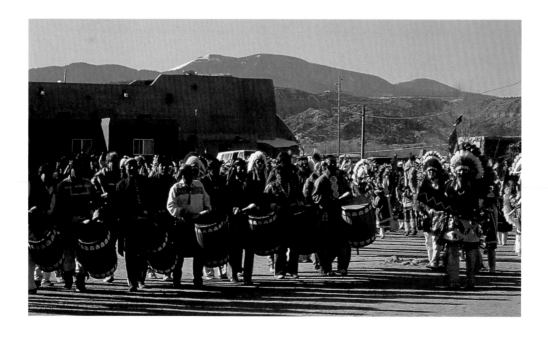

At the end of San Ildefonso's feast day, dancers reassemble on top of the kiva. Here, Timmy's father stands on the roof holding a flag. He is dressed in red. At sunset, the dancers reenter the kiva and get ready to go back to their everyday life.

Timmy is proud of his Indian heritage. He learns dances and songs that have been passed from father to son for 10,000 years. He also learns twentieth-century ways of life. At school he works with his computer and develops skills he will use in the future world.

Timmy likes to belong to two cultures. He feels he has the best of both worlds. When he grows up, Timmy—Star Fire—will also teach his children the Pueblo Indian ways that preserve the regular passing of the seasons and the fruitfulness of the earth.